Retired

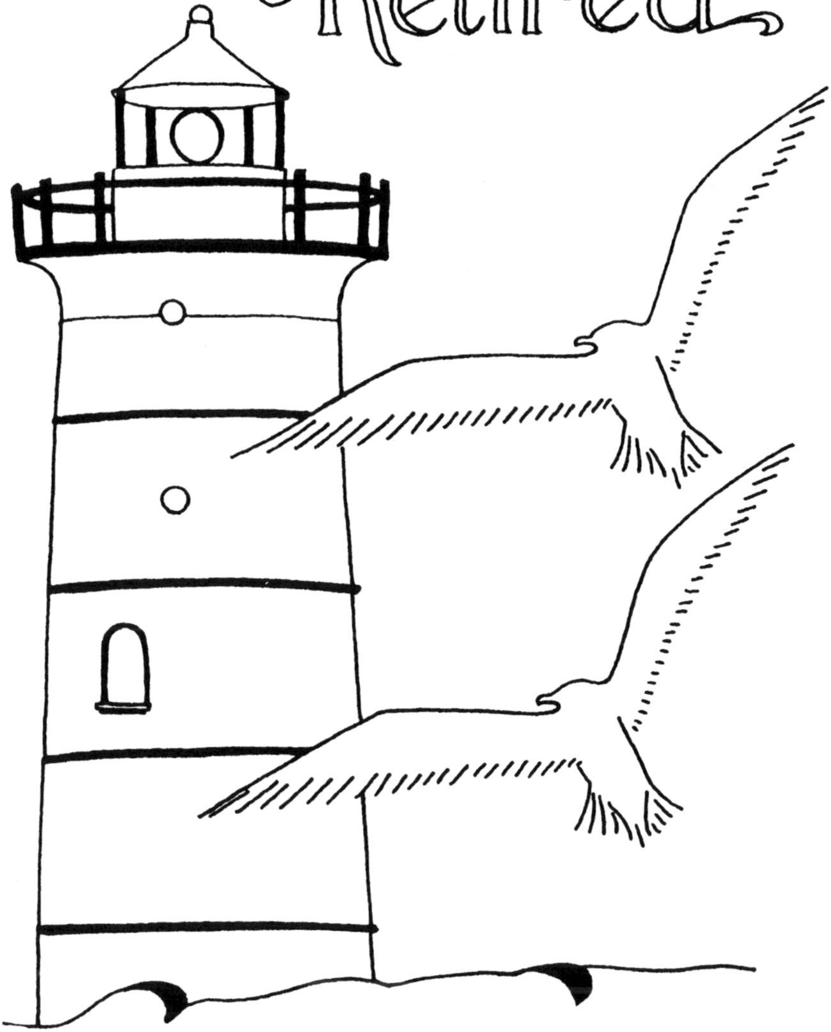

Donald R. Siegel
Jeanne R. Slavin Siegel

ISBN: 0-9644769-4-0

Library of Congress Control Number: 2002093986

Cover Illustration by Mary Vaupotic

Poetry on page 16 by Jack Detuca Gross

Printed in the United States by Morris Publishing
3212 East Highway 30 • Kearney, NE 68847
1-800-650-7888

RETIRED

A LIFE IN POETRY
MORE LIFE IN POETRY
FEATHERS
REMINISCE

Published in:

CHAPBOOKS
- The American Poetry Society
- Alms House Press

ANTHOLOGIES
- Iliad Press
- National Library of Poetry
- Sparrowgrass Poetry Press
- The Amherst Press
- Arcadia Poetry Press
- Creative Arts & Science
- Poets Guild
- Quill Books
- The Rift Magazine
- Armadillo Press
- Also published in Mainichi Daily News Tokyo, Japan

AWARDS
Certificates of Merit
- Iliad Press
- International Society of Authors & Artists

Editors Choice Award
- National Library of Poetry

Members of
- International Society of Poets
- The Academy of American Poets
- The New York Poetry Forum, Inc.
- Rockland Haiku Society
- The Traveling Ark--Poets of New Jersey

Born in New York City, we moved to New City, (Rockland County), New York in 1958. We are members of The International Society of Poets--The Academy of American Poets--The New York Poetry Forum, Inc.--Rockland County Haiku and The Traveling Ark of New Jersey. we have been published in many national and international anthologies. Jeanne received an award for First Place in the Mainichi Daily News of Tokyo, Japan for her haiku poetry. We have been featured readers in New York and New Jersey. We also conduct readings at The Northern Metropolitan Nursing Home and The Castle Point Veterans Hospital. We helped to create a Krystallnacht program at the Holocaust Museum & Study Center in Spring Valley, New York. This program will be featured in other areas of New York and New Jersey. This is our fifth book of poetry.

A Life In Poetry
More Life In Poetry
Feathers
Reminisce

RETIRED

CONTENTS

1--No Discrimination
2--Forty Seven Years
3--Clarkstown Lament
4--2001 Odyssey
5--Joys Of Winter
6--Grace Of God
7--Grace Of God--Page 2
8--Hair
9--Great Opera
10--Haiku And Five Line Tanka
11--Owl Talk
12--2484--Short Story
13--2484--Page 2
14--The Owl And A Friend
15--Changes
16--Some Are Seen To Me As Is
By Jack Deluca Gross
17--Grace Of God #2
18--Terminal
19--Ides Of March
20--Anticipation
21--Wait
22--Vacation--Again
23--The End
24--Dreams
25--A Thought (Sonnet)
26--How Do We Feel
27--Afternoon In June
28--The Barbecue
29--Reverie--An Essay
30--Henry Wadsworth Longfellow
31--Boscobel Restoration
32--Skye
33--Never On Sunday
34--Krystallnacht
35--A Meeting
36--Winds Of War
37--Untitled
38--Computer Age
39--Bored
40--Need To Write

CONTENTS

41--Mourners--Shiva Call
42--911--Emergency
43--Birth Of A Word
44--Constant Craving
45--God Bless America
46--Fifty Years Later
47--Retired
48--Greg Sikorsky
49--Forgotten
50--Haiku Poetry
51--Another Year
52--Krystallnacht--2001
53--Travels
54--Time To Move On
55--Predictions
56--Questions
57--Questions--Page 2
58--A New Year--2002
59--A Vermont Teddy Bear
60--Drowning--Not Yet
61--Doctor Luks
62--I Wish
63--Jeanne
64--Frustration
65--Creation--January 2002
66--Wondered
67--Seasons
68--Resulutions--2002
69--A Sentinel
70--What Was--What Is--What Will Be
71--Holidays
72--Spring
73--Cat
74--Finis
75--Waiting
76--Haiku Poetry
77--Our Magnolia Tree
78--Farting
79--Gobeldegook
80--The Long Wait

RETIRED CONTENTS

81--Arthur Avenue
82--Going Home
83--June 24, 2002--10PM
84--Post Mortem
85--I Wish
86--I Wish--Page 2
87--A Night In Provincetown

Poems By Jeanne Slavin Siegel

88--Winter Nightmare
89--Winter Nightmare--Page 2
90--Childrens View Of Christmas Eve
91--Childrens View Of Christmas Eve--Page 2
92--The Visitor
93--Seasonal Moods
94--Another Sunday
95--Stormy Meditations
96--Anticipation
97--The Arrival
98--The Routine
99--The Departure
100--The Tree From Hell
101--In A Class Of Its Own
102--The Stereotype
103--A Sterile World
104--Tuesday, September 11, 2001
105--California--Summer In The Desert
106--Haiku Poetry
107--Great Expectations
108--Forever Winter
109--A December Nightmare
110--Skye And Jake
111--August 14, 1990--June 24, 2002
112--1941
113--The Roses Of Cape Cod
114--Treasures Of The Past
115--Search And Find
116--Another Time--Another Place
117--Another Time--Another Place--Page 2
118--A Penny Postcard--A Book--A Life
119--A Penny Postcard--A Book--A Life--Page 2

NO DISCRIMINATION

Leaves--all sizes, shapes and
all different colors
gather on our lawn.

They play with the wind
and somersault with birds
then come to rest on our lawn.

After an autumn of play
they sleep on our lawn
till they awake with new purpose.

Spring arrives with a warm wind.
Animals run through the field
to wake all the leaves.

Leaves--all sizes, shapes and
all different colors
awake to become--fertilizer.

. . .

FORTY SEVEN YEARS

Forty seven years--
      a lifetime for some
just a beginning for us.

Time to celebrate the beginning
      commemorate the start
a lifetime together--never apart.

So much we've seen
      so much we've done
so much still left undone.

A new set of commands
      grandchildren make their demands
their lives starting anew.

Forty seven years--still counting
      children, grandchildren Tiffany and
I will love you--ALLWAYS.

Happy Anniversary.

.   .   .

CLARKSTOWN LAMENT

T'was the night before Christmas
and everything is the same.
The roads are still not paved
and the pot holes remain.

Our children are snug in their bed
when there is a sound that they dread.
Dad, home from a day of work
putting his car in the shed.

Pot holes he hollers with a shout
and women drivers all about.
The malls are filled to capacity
the clerks making sales with veracity.

914 for Westchester and Putnam remain
but for Rockland 845 is the game.
Even in Chappaqua where Clinton resides
914 is the area code that abides.

The lights are so bright
on this festive night.
We celebrate the joy of Christmas and Chanuka
the world over, even in Chappaqua.

Now as you go to your bed
fond thoughts fill your head
of a new Tappan Zee Bridge
and skiing in Westchester instead.

And I heard Santa exclaim
as he flew overhead--
"Take care with your skiing
a broken leg can be a dread."

. . .

2001--AN ODYSSEY

They came for me
      2 A.M. everything still dark.
They came in a stretch limousine
      my two friends
already waiting for me.
      They gave us pills--
our normal food of the day.
      Mine tasted like bacon and eggs
my friends had steak and potatoes
      soon we would be eating
the real food--no more pills.
      We stopped to pick up a woman.
I never saw her before.
      Now we were on our way.

The airport was crowded
      photographers taking pictures
reporters were everywhere.
      We were rushed into
a special elevator and then
      up, up, up for more than 100 feet.
Finally at a landing
      a small door opened.
We entered a spacious livingroom--
      capsules along the walls.
We were directed to our places
      given some pills and
asked to lie down.
      My pill tasted like an ice cream soda.

We all became very sleepy
      must have been drugged.
The only thing that I remember is
      a dream--travel to a distant planet
and cooking real food
      over an open fire.
It was an odyssey
      a far off trip to Atlantis
an adventure, or was it all
      just a dream--?
Then there was a baby born in--

      2001

JOYS OF WINTER

Foliage disappears and
    the starkness of winter
brings a new beauty to the land.

Animals scamper through the woods
    adding another dimension of color
and the hunter returns.

Snow soon covers it all
    white with some brown outcropping
and footprints where animals have been.

It snowed again
    snow upon snow upon snow.
I may never see our driveway again.

Freezing rain creates
    a jeweled forest but
the snow remains.

The trip to the supermarket
    becomes a hazardous experience
wearing clothes that weigh more than me.

Another joy of winter
    anticipation--
two more months 'til spring.

Buds long dormant
    burst into magnificant colors and
green replaces white.

Foliage, green leaves return
    to cover the trees
and the robin sings.

GRACE OF GOD

31st Regiment
    7th Division
        24th Corp
My outfit.

The great war
    was winding down
almost over but still
    there was work to do.

We traveled the Pacific
    finally arriving in Korea.
In 1948 we were sent to Hawaii.
    I went home--honorable discharge.

Just two years after that
    the call to serve again.
My unit--"L" Company--31st Regiment
    7th Division returned to Korea.

Triumphantly they marched
    past the Chosin Reservoir
almost to the Yalu River--
    the border of China.

Forty below zero, it was freezing
    how well I remember the cold.
North and South Korea almost united
    it was not meant to be.

Thirty thousand strong, the Chinese
    suddenly appeared.
They attacked our perimeter
    they would not be denied.

My outfit, the 31st Regiment
    fought gallantly but still
they had to retreat.
    They were overwhelmed.

GRACE OF GOD

Frozen, dead Chinese soldiers
    their bodies piled high
lined our path of retreat
    back to Hagaru-ri.

Even our wounded were
    killed by the advancing Chinese.
Back through Sinhu then Hudong-ni
    and then at Hagaru-ri,
the 31st was no more.

Many of my friends died
    in that fateful retreat but
through the grace of God
    I was not one of them.

Often wondering
    now, after fifty one years--
I finally find out about friends--
    lives wasted in a fruitless war.

. . .

HAIR

Darling, they are growing old
     silver threads among the bold
hair that survived the cold.

Haircream could not destroy
     that 3" pompadour--OH BOY!

What's past is past
     what's done is done
the hair didn't last but
     memories--we sure had fun.

Now once more around town
     a new life begun.
Poetry written with scowl or frown
     and no new hair to be undone.

So, here's to the new year--2001
     memories still being written
children and grandchildren
     we're still having fun.

. . .

GREAT OPERA

Instruments are tuned
    the conductor waves his baton
and the orchestra comes to life.

Slow and melodic
    then fast and furious
the final crescendo.

A new soprano arrives
    red faced and hairless as
the conductor waves the umbilical cord.

The aria, sung in high "C"
    composed by Mr. and Mrs. and
transcribed by Ms. Soprano.

Libretto on request.

. . .

HAIKU AND 5 LINE TANKA

Lacy snowflakes
crocheted by angels
fall on my nose.

In our cellar
owl fell down chimney
smells like chicken.

Cholestrol warning
only one egg allowed
mine has two yokes.

Siamese cat
greets another siamese cat
with a hiss.

Faucet breaks and
air conditioner breaks and
I broke.

Six thousand people
in two buildings
a sudden crematorium
love lasts as people die
the devil came to visit.

Standing and watching
the deer standing and watching
then he shoots.

Buck
searches for doe
object fawn.

. . .

OWL TALK

An owl came to play
    in our cellar one day.
Down our chimney he flew
    as he hollers, "Who--Who."

"I know who"
    said the chipmunk with alarm,
"You flew down the chimney
    to do me some harm."

Even the mouse scurried about
    and with loud voice he gave a shout,
"I'm too young to die today.
    So why don't you just fly away."

Our cat came to see what was the matter
    as owl, chipmunk and mouse all scatter.
My workbench was turned asunder
    with a noise that sounded like thunder.

Never leave your chimney uncovered.
    You too may one day discover
an owl that flew in to play
    and "Who--Who" is all he would say.

2484

In 1990 people were concerned about global warming. They tried to do something about it but nations would not cooperate. Since there was little to be done on earth, they began to explore space. Scientists were looking for radio signals or any sign of life, extra terrestrials, aliens, UFO's, anything that might lead to another place to live. In the 1990's they already knew that life on earth could not go on. These were brave people living in space stations with their primitive modes of travel. Gradually they began to improve. The great celebration in 2312 when the millionth person was living in a space station and even the colony living on Mars were all milestones. Meanwhile earth continued to destabilize. Global warming could no longer be controled.

Global warming began to take its toll. The ice at the North and South Poles had melted so much that the earth could no longer maintain its orbit. Because of the many earthquakes, the gas escaping from the center of the earth and the floods, our atmosphere was being poisoned. The earth was no longer habitable. The underground shelters were not satisfactory. There would have to be a mass migration, but where could everyone go? There were so few space ships and so many people.

All of the years of space exploration might finally prove itself. We knew about seventeen possible places to go to. There were stars that were similar to our sun with planets orbiting them. They were solar systems. We have already explored one of these solar systems closest to earth. The planet far enough from their sun, similar to our earth, was abandoned probably for the same reason that we will have to abandon earth. Still, there was evidence of an advanced civilization that had lived there.

Our space ships were poised from every angle on earth, for immediate takeoff. They were loaded with provisions for a long flight. There were also tapes, books, scientific equipment and everything that would remind them of earth. The people knew that they would never be able to return. Because of all the equipment, there was room for only two or four people at the most in each space ship. All of the ships were programmed for a different solar system. Hopefully, some of them would get through. They were all waiting for the signal, ignition, and they would be off. All of the remaining people on earth seemed to be resigned to their fate. They were taking trips, that long planned for vacation, buying that new car, or doing things that they always wanted to do. People were no longer planning for any tomorrow.

The earth began shaking violently. It seemed to be oscillating at a much greater speed. Finally, almost too late, the signal came. Some of the space ships crashed on takeoff. Earthquakes cracked their takeoff platforms. The majority of them did get away.

One after the other, signals came to earth of failures. Apparently there was nothing out there. Only one report came in that was favorable. The ship found a planet that had the proper atmosphere. There was plenty of water, vegetation, some small animals and even an unattended apple orchard. Unfortunately, there were only two people on this space ship, a man and a woman.

. . .

THE OWL AND A FRIEND

The owl, harbinger of life
    or death
came to visit but not to stay.

Is he wise with glaring eye
    or just a fool
fell down our chimney to die.

We sent him out to fly away
    help to control our environment
and return to us another day.

A friend died today.
    She came to know us 23 years ago
but she couldn't stay.

Wish that she could fly away
    (she was too young to die)
and return to us another day.

. . .

CHANGES

Constantly changing
    everything changes
even ocean tides change
    as does the shoreline.

Homes that lined the shore
    slowly disappear.
Last year's shoreline
    becomes this year's beach.

Even the whale
    breaching on the horizon
becomes confused as
    his horizon comes closer to shore.

New York City, also constantly changing,
    changes as the ocean
with tides of different people
    entering and leaving.

Neighborhoods, so familiar with
    family restaurants, quaint odors and
beautiful old-fashioned theaters,
    all change, they move with the tide.

Slums replace
    what were new buildings then and
the streets look older.

Now, as I return to the old neighborhood
    searching for friends, old buildings,
the old theater where we used to see
    2 pictures, 11 cartoons and no porn,
I walk the streets of my youth
    and I realize--
you can't return.

. . .

Dedicated to Don Siegel
& Jeanne Slavin Siegel
and their trip to the U.K. 2001,
and their return trip to their trappings
here in the U.S. and here in our hearts too us,

some are seen to me as is...
"For Don and Jeanne"
by Jack DeLuca Gross

...You May Be Going Away For A Fortnight
Going Away From My Spyglass Sight For Now
But You Still Will Stay Behind In Bold Site
Alongside And Inside My Heart's Light For Now
In Traces Of Thought Mindful, Full In My Mind's Eye
In The Places Of Prayer Soulful, Full In My Soul's See
Till The Day You Both Bring Yourselves Home And Come Back To Me
Until When I See The Way You Were Again The Way You Are Seen
Please Take Care For Now Please Remain Safe And Sound All Around
Until Your Returns Take Place From Sea To See In Poems Of Poetry...
...some are seen to me as is always
even when away from the see of me.

JDG / Pen Is Press
2001 Rochelle Park, N.J.
#031001

JDG

GRACE OF GOD--2

At the nursing home
    they congregate--
senior citizens all--
    this is their home.

They are fed
    they are dressed
they are cleaned
    when they have messed.

Day in and day out
    they scamper about
no place to go, nothing to do
    they look out of windows
hoping to see you.

Once a month they gather
    anxiously waiting for us
to share our poetry with them
    bringing back memories
of yesteryear.

I watch their faces
    they laugh, they cry
some with a vacant stare
    who knows what they are thinking of.

We are finished reading
    two hours of joy for all and
I can't help but wonder--
    there but for the Grace of God go I.

. . .

TERMINAL

Terminal--a train station where
people gather waiting for
that shiny new train that
takes them to a vacation wonderland.

Terminal--an airport where
people wait for
that huge airplane that takes them to
an exotic land--vacation.

Terminal--a disease--cancer
pain and suffering preclude
drugs--horrible treatments and
ultimate death with few exceptions.

Terminal--a cousin--
young with sudden cancer.
Treatments, torturous drugs, pain and
--terminal.

Terminal--a life--
young or old
live your life the best that you can
tomorrow might be--terminal.

. . .

IDES OF MARCH

You are so nasty
     you always run away from me.
We never talk
     never go out to play
never even go out to walk together.

They say you are prejudiced
     but I don't believe it.
I don't believe in prejudice.
     I even like some of your friends.
I would just like to be friends with you.

Please let bygones be bygones.
     It is springtime, let's be friends.
Won't you come to my home to visit
     said the fox to the hare.

. . .

ANTICIPATION

All our lives seem to consist of--
    anticipation--remembrance and
anticipation again.
    Where is contentment--acceptance--
this is where we are.

Minutes are like hours
    waiting for the limousine
that takes us to Kennedy Airport.
    It's been a year since
we last saw our son and his family.

Picturing how they have grown and
    if they still remember us and
if we can keep up with our grandchildren--
    suddenly we are startled by a horn,
the limousine is here.

Four suitcases, two carry-on pieces
    and us all crowded together--
we are off.
    Once more anticipation and
a prayer for a safe flight.

Tomorrow we will be in
    Manchester, England.

. . .

WAIT

We arrived three hours early for our flight
     checked in our luggage
and found a nice place to sit--read
     and wait, and wait, and wait.

The weather is bad, it is raining and
     strong winds are predicted.
I hope we will be able to leave and
     I pray for a safe flight.

The call to board the airplane
     came just in time--
five minutes before I would scream
     I can't wait anymore.

Within thirty minutes
     everyone was comfortably seated
our luggage was secured and
     we wait, and we wait, and we wait.

Forty planes are ahead of us
     waiting to take off
for places all over the world and
     we wait for ninety minutes more.

Airborn--a six hour forty minute flight
     takes forever and guess what--
the weather is bad--it is raining, cold--
     strong winds--Manchester,England
this is where we came in.

We leave the warm sun
     sitting on top of the clouds
and descend through horrible weather
     for a perfect landing.

There is a mad rush
     to get off the plane and
rush to the carousel
     and wait for our luggage.
     .   .   .

VACATION--AGAIN

A year went by
     since we were here--
such a long time but
     now that we are here
it seems like it was only yesterday.

Little hands and
     cold little feet
make being here
     an early morning treat.

Like an elaborate prepared meal
     hours if not days to prepare
then over with in one dinner and
     forgotten in one week.

This vacation visiting our son, his wife and
     grandchildren young and beautiful
--a year in preparation
     over so soon--never forgotten.

. . .

THE END

Once more anticipation--
    a safe flight
the limousine should arrive on time
    and our luggage also.
Soon we will be home.

Skye, Jake, Christopher--
    grandchildren so far apart
every child's voice gives me a start.
    Anticipation--our daughter also waits
and prays for our safe return.

As we begin our approach--
    Kennedy Airport looks so beautiful.
I'm looking forward to seeing our daughter--
    Tiffany our cat--home--and
anticipation--another year to wait.

. . .

DREAMS

Today I had a dream.
I dreamt about yesterday--
trips to far away places and
things seen, never forgotten.

I dreamt about Spain, Italy
the Vatican and Israel--
family, cousins and a life
not seen for so many years.

Yesterday I had a dream.
I dreamt about tomorrow--
a cure for cancer, AIDS and
peace in the world.

I dreamt about new airplanes
flying wings with 800 passengers and
space ships--daily commuters
to distant planets.

I dreamt about grandchildren and
the type of life they will lead.
I can't help but wonder how much
of their lives we will be able to share.

I am looking out of our front window.
Our magnolia tree is in full bloom and
Tiffany our cat, sitting in my lap, assures me
it will be a good year.

A THOUGHT--(SONNET)

When I have fears
that I might cease to be
I think of all that I hold dear
and all that I might never see.

I think of travel to distant lands
England, Italy and family in Israel.
Nine new cousins are in that band
a scene that will be unreal.

Grandchildren are always on my mind
how quick they all grow.
Their education--their lives may be a grind
there is so much more they have to know.

Family and grandchildren, so much to enjoy
I put my fears aside and share in their joy.

. . .

HOW DO WE FEEL

With apprehension and love
we plan to meet friends.
After a long hiatus, it has been
eight years since we last met.

Today we met our friends
their lives entwined with ours.
We have shared our lives--
past, present and future too.

There is so much to share
so much that has transpired.

Our children have become adults and
their children--our grandchildren
are all so much older but still
our friends have not aged.

The same in thought and spirit
even the invasion of the computer
lap top and cell phone
has not changed them.

Eight years since we last met
so much has changed.
Tape decks, tape cassettes and
the console T-V are all gone.

Days, years--our lives
pass by so quick
we don't have time
to remember our friends.

Time to leave, we kiss--we hug
with tears in our eyes
we make a promise
next year we will all meet again.

. . .

AFTERNOON IN JUNE

Clouds slowly move
     making room
for trees to touch the sky.

I look up and watch
     clouds--different shapes
stories to be told.

I see my son--his wife
     grandchildren all returned
so far away--still they are near.

My daughter gave birth
     to a business
a star shining in the daytime.

My wife shares my view
     even though we are retired
there is so much more to do.

Travel, Broadway Shows and
     the gym is a must.
Writing poetry is necessary too.

Sky touching the treetops
     lights up the day and
lights my way.

.   .   .

THE BARBECUE

Charcoal--lighter fluid
    everything just right
bring on the London broil
    smothered in garlic.

As I sit on our rear deck
    with only the sounds
of our neighborhood
    our little jungle
begins to come to life.

I place the meat on the barbecue
    while everyone watches.
Rabbits, squirrels and even an owl
    stare hungrily.

Now the long wait
    fortified with a glass of Scotch
while everything cooks
    just right.

A bluejay--head held high
    wings slowly reversing
gracefully lands in our field
    and walks toward the barbecue.

A rabbit--nose twitching
    with a mouth full of grass
not interested she would say
    as she scampers away.

Leaves always moving
    as many eyes watch me
a squirrel sails from tree to tree and
    big brown eyes
a deer stares through the leaves.

Now the London broil and the scotch
    are both done.
The woods become quiet as I move--
    it is dinner time.

. . .

REVERIE--AN ESSAY

SUNDAY, JUNE 17, 2001, IT IS FATHERS DAY. I SIT HERE WATCHING, BUT NOT REALLY WATCHING, THE TELEVISION. I DON'T KNOW IF I WAS ASLEEP OR IF SOME MEMORIES INVADED MY REVERIE. I SEE MOM CRYING AS I WENT OFF TO WAR. I SENT A PICTURE HOME WITH MY RIGHT HAND BEHIND MY BACK. IN HER NEXT LETTER THE FIRST QUESTION WAS HOW BAD WAS I HURT. HOW PROUD DAD WAS WHEN I CAME HOME. IT WAS LIKE A HOLIDAY.

OUR WEDDING, CHILDREN, OUR HOME IN THE COUNTRY. IT ALL SEEMS LIKE A DREAM. A DREAM OF YESTERDAY. MY INLAWS--NO, THAT IS TOO COLD. THEY WERE PARENTS TO ME ALSO. NOW OUR PARENTS ARE ALL GONE. HOW I REALLY MISS ALL OF THEM. I WONDER WHAT POP AND NANNA AND MY PARENTS WOULD THINK IF THEY KNEW THAT NOW WE WRITE POETRY AND HAVE SO MANY BOOKS PUBLISHED. I KNOW THAT THEY WOULD HAVE BEEN PROUD OF US.

BEAUTIFUL MEMORIES CONTINUE TO RETURN AS I SIT IN OUR DEN WITH MY BEAUTIFUL WIFE AND WE WATCH T-V AT THE END OF A VERY NICE DAY.

I LOVE YOU.

HENRY WADSWORTH LONGFELLOW

Henry Wadsworth Longfellow
     wrote poetry long ago.
He had a message to impart--
     some things we ought to know.

More than 200 years ago
     he painted scenes so vivid
of the blacksmith, the sailing boat
     and Paul Revere too.

We read about a time unknown
     and once more we can return
to a land of strife--
     by todays standards--a very hard life.

Now I can say goodnight to Mr. Longfellow
     and put his verse to bed
till we meet again by candle glow
     tomorrow night instead.

. . .

BOSCOBEL RESTORATION*

WALKING IN THE GARDEN
AMONG ALL DIFFERENT SHAPES AND SHADES OF
ROSES, MARIGOLDS AND EVEN PANSIES
AND AN OCCASIONAL SQUIRREL
SCURRYING THROUGH THE BRUSH
AS I ENJOY A GLASS OF WINE
AT THE BOSCOBEL HOME
RESTORED FOR FAMILY AND FRIENDS AND
SHAKSPEARE CAME TO VISIT
WITH HIS ENTOURAGE OF
CHRISTIAN NOBILITY AND EVEN
A JEW FROM VENICE.**

. . .

*GARRISON, NEW YORK
**MERCHANT OF VENICE

SKYE

I would like to write a poem
     about an eight year old
girl with blue eyes, blonde hair and
     a mouth beyond compare.

Her actions can be a treat
     when she wakes us with
her little cold feet.

On her scooter she is a terror
     as people run for shelter
into the nearest cellar.

War with her brother
     she will foment and
with her parents
     she will torment.

Exasperation is the feeling
     but then--a hug, a kiss
we love you little miss.

.   .   .

NEVER ON SUNDAY

Go to the bank, post office
    even the mall but
NEVER ON SUNDAY.

Hurting from an accident
    need a doctor, dentist but
NEVER ON SUNDAY.

Drive the highway to
    museums and a show but
NEVER ON SUNDAY.

Death--an injury
    call the priest but
NEVER ON SUNDAY.

Need to relax
    call a prostitute but
NEVER ON SUNDAY.

Not on Wednesday either.

. . .

KRYSTALLNACHT*

GOD cried--people died
People died and GOD cried
Night of the devil
Devils night
End of the beginning
Beginning of the end
When earth stood still
People slept OUR lives away
Day ends--nightmare begins
Apocalypse then
Goodness disappears--evil appears.

. . .

*Night Of The Broken Glass

A MEETING

A look
A stare
     so familiar

A word
A name
     a tear

A place
Remembering
A cousin
A brother
     an embrace

Auschwitz
They were spared
     thank GOD

.   .   .

WINDS OF WAR

A tunnel of green
    begins to disappear as
the leaves of September
    now multi-colored and sparse
greet the Nazi
    invaders of Poland and
a long cold winter begins.

Even the weeping willow
    tree with long branches
reaching to the ground
    begins to cry.

Birds can no longer sing
    deer can not laugh
only the sound of the raucous crow
    can be heard through the land
giving harsh orders.

. . .

UNTITLED

It is said that
     not to remember--to forget
is to be condemned to repeat
     the Holocaust again.

Now after 63 years--
     once again a situation--
Israel at the brink and
     Jews being wantonly killed--
will it ever end?

We must remain militarily strong
     psychologically vigilant
and passionately free.

Now, as I sit in
     an Arab restaurant
in a possible hostile
     Arab neighborhood in Brooklyn
writing poems about Israel
     and talking to Muslim Arabs--
we seem to have an understanding
     and we are at peace.

I wonder if we can package and
     export this peace
to the Palestinians and Israel.

. . .

COMPUTER AGE

It was a long struggle.
We fought, we ignored
we reveled in
our computer ignorance
to no avail.
I knew the battle was lost
when we couldn't open our E Mail.

So welcome to the computer age
with reckless motorists
harassing police and
rude people, impatient--
no time, always rushing
to get home to that grinning face
on their computer screen.

It has won
it has taken over
mind and body--the people.
It directs--controls
all intelligence--even emotions
are controlled by their computers.

Planet of the computer
how complex we have become.
Now with blank faces
people are walking aimlessly
no greetings--no talking
just a blank stare.
They look at the sky and
down at the street.
What can they do now--
their computer is down.

. . .

BORED

They are crawling
     up and down my arm.
Little insects so small
     they can't even be seen.

Even my eyes begin
     twitching as I watch
the television with no picture--
     not even turned on.

Torn cartilage--
     I just had an operation.
Arthroscopic surgery
     over so quick
and now I can't even dance.

Next there are months of therapy
     massages and exercise.
While everything is progressing
     I'm still bored.

. . .

NEED TO WRITE

Apocalypse now
    our years are flying by
till the end.

Minutes--days--even years
    disappear into the sunset
of another era.

We have to keep writing
    adding more pages
to our story of
    love--life--and our future.

. . .

<u>MOURNERS--SHIVA* CALL</u>

Person mourning
     sitting on a carton
surrounded by family
     and some friends.

They sit--they talk
     a stolen glance
then they rise--move about
     to another place
and sit and talk.

So much candy--
     so much cake--
if not for my diet
     everything would be Jake.

Just one more bite
     It's time to say good night.
Another stolen glance
     a kiss--a hug--a tear.

. . .

*Jewish mourning period

911--EMERGENCY*

Airplanes crash
    debris everywhere and
buildings fall.

An accident
    no--too perfect
a plan.

Terrorists and death
    everywhere
death from terrorists.

Pay the piper--
    piper must be paid
retribution is on the way.

A nation far away
    their capitol city aflame and
a statement--PAID IN FULL.

Terrorists die
    amid new destruction
while people continue to cry.

. . .

*September 11, 2001

BIRTH OF A WORD

Holocaust--
born in German hell
nurtured on Jewish blood
then fed to the world.

They brewed it in Kosovo
tried it in Iraq and
fed it to the Kurds.

Gypsies hated it--
Irish gave up on it and
the Basques packaged it and
returned it to sender.

It had to be worked on--
change the meaning and
increase the letters to include
terror, holocaust, terrorists.

Arabs worked on it and
experimented in Israel.
When they thought they had it right
they brought it to the United States.

The United States didn't want it.
They had to erase the words--
holocaust and terrorist.

These words--born so long ago
tried very hard to survive.

The first words to be eliminated
in the twenty first century
will be holocaust--terrorist and
all people that try to use them.

Two obelisks--two new twin towers
will rise to touch the clouds
and on their windows there will be
images of all those
people that lived there before and
will still live forever
in these new obelisks that
reach up to GOD.

. . .

CONSTANT CRAVING

Cholestrol special--
    steak, eggs and home fries
vacation time--breakfast.

Another thought--
    another poem--
creation--one more time.

A show--an opera and
    enough money to afford
a life--our life.

Another month--
    another year--
till 120 years--a life.

. . .

GOD BLESS AMERICA

It was a beautiful day
with only our poetry to read today.
Music--dancing--singing--
God Bless America.

Another day--another problem
today it's the plumbing
yesterday it was my knee
tomorrow--who knows--
still we live in a land that is free.
God Bless America.

Terrorists attack and
we fight back.
Our soldiers fight the good fight
also suffering and possible death
to allow us to remain free.
God Bless America.

Depression begins to take hold
I don't know what to do
still I'm happy being here with you
in this land that is free.
God Bless America.

From the mountains
to the prairies
even the oceans have their problems.
This land--the greatest
will always be free.
God Bless America.

GOD BLESS AMERICA

. . .

FIFTY YEARS LATER

We commemorate--celebrate
    the night of broken glass
call to attention
    liberation of the camps
celebrate the end of the war
    end of the destruction of a people.

Why do we commemorate
    these acts of horror
why do we celebrate
    these days of remembrance
why do we remind the world
    of days--years--of the Holocaust.

Do we have to remind everyone of
    days when the earth stood still
people stood still
    did nothing to try to help--
when the conscience of the world
    burned in flames of the Holocaust.

Yes, we do have to remind the world
    continually remind the people
lest they begin to forget--
    allow complacency to rule their lives
remind them of what was and
    what could still be.

NEVER AGAIN.

. . .

RETIRED

Like a blanket
     clouds drift by
with many different shapes
     covering a bed of blue
hanging like trophies
     above my roof.

I rest on my hammock
     watching the squirrels
scampering through a tomato patch
     while rabbits are trying to eat
lunch in the afternoon
     of another boring day.

Birds are always so busy
     building their nests and
feeding their young.

Buds are beginning to burst
     and flowers
all with brilliant colors
     are blooming.

My book
     with a shiny cover is
now lying on the ground
     reflecting the clouds
with many different shapes
     hanging like trophies
above my outside roof.

I sleep
     and poems of yesterday
float in my head
     as I dream lazily
of tomorrow--bored.

I still want to fly
     sex every night
perhaps in the morning too and
     travel to distant lands
dance the tango
     not only in my dreams--

. . .

GREG SIKORSKY*

Today we said goodbye
    to a man
        to a way of life
to a family no longer complete.

A home--a room completed
    a new stone wall
his essence lives on.

Thirty five years or
    one hundred twenty years
however long it takes
    to live a life
he will not be forgotten.

. . .

*Fireman lost in September 11, 2001
catastrophe

FORGOTTEN

They look at me
    and then walk by.
Some, their eyes half closed
    look at the sky.

They look at the inscription
    upon the stone
relieved that I was not known.

Then they stop
    a tear hits the ground.
They look, they stare,
    they don't make a sound.

Then they say their prayer
    it sounds like music
in my lair.

Why are no stones
    placed on my head?
Don't they remember
    I am dead?

. . .

HAIKU POETRY

SEPTEMBER 11, 2001

Love-life and death
all partners--
the devil came to visit.

Six thousand people
in two buildings
a sudden crematorium
love lasts as people die
the devil came to visit.

One whiff and one sniff
and six months to recover
anthrax discovered.

Napalm bomb
on top of Bin Laden
he smelled like chicken.

. . .

ANOTHER YEAR

The master painter
     adds beautiful colors
to our green leaves
     as fall arrives.

Yellow, red, orange and brown
     leaves of every color
decorate our trees and our lawn.

Everything dormant
     animals and trees
prepare for a long sleep.
     Soon it will be winter.

Deer with fuzzy antlers and
     squirrels with long bushy tails
and even chipmunks hurry
     to prepare for winter.

A black and white world
     with everything frozen and bleak
awaits the end of
     a catastrophic year.

New words--Taliban, terrorist
     al-Qaida, Bin Laden
destruction, trauma and death
     invade our daily thoughts.

For me the new year begins
     when animals and even trees
awaken to new life
     and the robin sings.

. . .

KRYSTALLNACHT--2001

We tried to tell them.
We tried to get them to listen.
Peace in the new millennium--not yet.
Krystallnacht--2001
The new Krystallnacht with
thousands dead and
buildings destroyed--
they didn't listen.
They couldn't hear.
They wouldn't understand.
Now, with rockets
missiles and mortar
once again children cry
and mothers weep.

. . .

TRAVELS

Today I found a pen*
a ball point pen
all alone in the world--
traveled from Germany
to meet new family and
left all alone
in West Nyack, New York
abandoned.
I put it in my inside pocket.

Strange how it clings
to my inside pocket and
vibrates when I take it
to write a poem
about traveling to distant lands
Spain, France and possibly
a return to Germany
to start all over again.

Visualizing this adventure
I would want to go
with this pen
to make sure that
it arrived safely.
I would want to travel
with this pen
in my inside pocket and
perhaps after the trip
I would adopt this pen
and return with it
to Rockland County, New York.

. . .

*Made in Germany

TIME TO MOVE ON

Twin Towers--110 floors--
    six thousand lives--
all destroyed--gone forever.

For the first time in 170 years
    like an invading army
terrorists arrive.

Suicide bombers--bacterial warfare
    the horrors of this new type of war
attack our way of life--our existence.

Trauma, heartache, loss of life
    everything must be put in its place.
It is time to move on.

We can't continue to write about this--
    recall the horror--
relive the tears.

Time to move on.
    Holidays--Hanukkah, Christmas
and a New Year approaches.

New buds, plants, animals and
    even people born in freedom--
God Bless America.

. . .

PREDICTIONS

Nostradamus predicted the end of the world in the year 2000. Fortunately he was wrong. Perhaps I can predict how the world will be in the third millennium. There will be small atomic wars that will destroy large sections of the Middle East. Even the United States will not be spared. Missiles capable of destroying entire cities will be used by every country. Countries that have only one missile will not hesitate to use it. The world will be a far different place than what we see today. With devastating wars and earthquakes the atmosphere will no longer support life.

At about the year 2400, underground cities will start to be built. They will be self contained with their own utilities and support systems. All vegetation will be cultivated in huge community farms underground. Advances in science will create an atmosphere similar to the outside world (not known to new generations). The average life span will be 150 years. People will not age as they do today. There will be no more old age syndrome. Most all body parts will be available for replacement without any rejection. People will be able to remain active until they just stop functioning. Death will be an instantaneous action not with prolonged pain. After 150 years of life, people will still look good without cosmetic adjustments.

We will be able to travel by atomic sleds through underground tunnels even to Europe. By the year of 3000 everything will be complete. In these tunnels, strip malls will be available at 750 mile intervals with rest stops at shorter intervals. All of the finest clothes, restaurants and entertainment centers will be located at every strip mall. The largest mall will be located in the center of the Atlantic Ocean, twelve miles deep.

Because of the great speeds of new airplanes, the sky will be reserved for interplanetary vehicles. There will also be space platforms that will contain everything a strip mall has plus security stations and fuel depots. All nations will be controlled by a World Federation similar to the present United Nations.

There will be a world at peace.

There will be a universe at peace.

. . .

QUESTIONS

How many years
do we have
allocated to us?

Do we just stop--
everything shuts down
and we die or--

Does each part
shut down separately
and we die little by little?

First the legs--necrosis
a bone in my knee
slowly dying.

I'm not ready for this.

I watch our trees
brown and dull green--
dingy looking.

I'm thinking--dreaming
about new life--
Springtime in Greenwich Village.

Walking the streets
enjoying the people
and the food.

Shows and the opera
in New York City
waiting to be seen by us.

Everything new and alive--
our tree eight inches taller
with bright green leaves and
a family of black squirrels frolicking.

Monday, Tuesday, Thursday and Friday
going to the gym
for our strenuous workout.

QUESTIONS--Page 2

Our daily--weekly routine
year after year with friends--
is this the year that it ends?

The big battle is beginning--
a battle against depression and
I must win--we will win.

Through poetry, deep breaths
meditation and my beautiful wife
we shall overcome.

Our lives are not ending
they are just beginning--
the second time around.

I am looking forward to--

grandchildren, shows, opera, the gym,
poetry to write, friends to visit,
walking the streets in Greenwich Village,
that old book store on Crosby Street--
so much left to do with
my beautiful wife.

I love you Jeanne.

. . .

A NEW YEAR--2002

Why am I being punished--
     placed in God's prison--
what did I do wrong?

I don't expect much--
     just some of lifes simplest pleasures
to be able to walk--talk--and write.

Thirty days--that is the sentence.
     Then the trail (operation) and
therapy will be the penalty.

There is one conslation.
     Serving the time with my wife
we will wake to a better day.

The sun will shine and
     the new year will be fine
through God's grace.

. . .

A VERMONT TEDDY BEAR

Surgery on my knee and
    I can't walk.
Sitting on our couch--I need help.

A Teddy Bear
    came all the way from Vermont
and sitting on an adjacent couch
    stares at me.

As I sit with my problems
    I return the stare and
a miracle happens--
    the Teddy Bear begins to breath.

He squirms--head going from side to side
    and our Vermont Teddy Bear
begins to stand and dance.

He stares and seems to be talking and
    I return the stare and then
eyes heavy, I begin to doze.

When I wake our Vermont Teddy Bear
    has returned to his place, sleeping.
I watch him and I feel better.

. . .

DROWNING--NOT YET

I wake to early morning waves--
    waves of depression
crashing on the shore
    of our daily lives.
I feel as if I am drowning.

The sun begins to shine and
    I rise to a new day--
a day full of expectations of
    what wonderful things
there might be for my wife and me.

The day progress and
    friends visit--people call
but to no avail.
    Waves of depression
continue to assail my shore.
    Again I feel like I am drowning.

I must keep my head above water.
    I don't want to drown.
My beautiful Jeanne
    is helping me to swim
against the rising tide
    of depression.

The weather is supposed to be mild.
    A prediction--waves will subside--
depression will disappear and
    my Jeanne and I
will go dancing again--
    God willing.

There is a rainbow
    on the other side of this page.
I am looking for it--
    desperately looking for the rainbow.

. . .

DOCTOR LUKS

We are born--
    we live our lives--
and we die.

There are only so many years
    granted to everyone
to live and to love.

I don't want to waste
    any moment, day, week
nor any year of our lives.

I don't have time to waste
    there is so much left undone--
so much more to do.

So hurry up Doctor Luks
    get this show on the road.
Please help me to walk.

I still want to
    walk with the animals
play ball with our grandchildren and
    dance with my Jeanne.

. . .

I WISH

I wish that I could sleep
sleep and dream
dream of February
February of the year 2002.

Snow would all be melting
melting and washing away
washing away memories
memories of our physical problems.

No more operations
operations that require therapy
therapy that will help me to walk
to walk to our new car.

I wish that I could wake
wake to a bright new day
a new day with sun shining
shining on my wife and I.

The gym beckons
beckons with our friends waiting
waiting for us to return
return to our way of life--again.

The world of poets
poets call for our return
return to a world of love and caring
caring to walk to the podium
and share feelings.

I wish that we could walk
walk down the street of dreams
dreams of Broadway--bright lights
bright lights--bright hopes--
our future.

. . .

JEANNE

How can I tell
    how much I love you?
You make the sun rise
    I am all aglow.

You light up my life
    remind me how lucky I am
to be allowed to share
    our lives together--precious and rare.

When I give you a scare
    I feel your care
with all of our problems
    we still love and share.

Tomorrow is a new day--
    a new year too.
It is time to resolve problems and
    never forget how much I love you.

So here's to our future--
    so much left to do--
opera and dancing and
    visiting grandchildren too.

The sun sets on an old year
    all things bad and blue
as the moon rises calling us
    to start our lives anew.

Therapy--maybe, operation--maybe
    once more the sun will rise
again I will be all aglow and
    you will still light up our lives.

It will be a new year
    a great year and
everything for us will be great
    God willing.

. . .

FRUSTRATION

My knee bothers me
  it is very unstable and
I would like to walk to my car
  but I can't do it--frustration.

Copies of my poems--shopping for food and
  a trip to the Post Office--
all necessary stops
  but I can't do it--frustration.

It snowed last night
  only two inches
no trouble to shovel the driveway
  but I can't do it--frustration.

Operation on my knee and then
  more problems--same knee and
another possible operation--help to walk
  I can't take this--frustration.

Frustrate--frustrated--frustration and
  a trip through the tunnel of life.
There is a light at the end of the tunnel and
  an end to frustration.

Life begins again
  at the end of the tunnel.
We are racing through this tunnel to the end
  Jeanne will be with me there.

. . .

CREATION--JANUARY 2002

The master creator
    creates diamond crystals--
multi-faceted all white
    beautiful diamond crystals.

They descend
    covering a world of horror
terrorists, death, destruction and
    world wide depression.

Even footprints of rabbits
    squirrels and birds
all disappear under new snow
    still searching for food.

A new world will emerge
    clean, fresh and unspoiled.
We will be there waiting--
    hopefully waiting.

. . .

WONDERED

I have often wondered
    how many more years
we would be allowed to go to the gym--
    to continue as we age--gracefully
to be able to share with friends
    poetry--stories of our lives.

I have often wondered
    why old people drag their feet.
Body functions begin to shut down.
    They walk so slow, talk slow and
so much has become difficult for them.
    Are they learning--preparing to die?

As the end of days
    continues to draw nearer
I have often wondered--

I am not ready to learn how to die.
    I am still in the process of
learning how to live.
    Please God, give us the time
to learn--

. . .

SEASONS

Springtime was such fun
    going on long hikes
hunting--sleeping in deer beds
    movies--shows and
dancing till dawn.

Summertime--the best time
    I survived high school, college
teenage years and then
    the army--death and destruction and
home to start life again.

Marriage--children--business
    even a new home.
The world is going so fast
    I don't have time--
must keep up.

Summertime--the best time of life
    certainly the most active
followed by Autumn
    leaves fall--hair falls and
children, now grown, leave home
    to start their lives--
the cycle continues.

As Autumn begins to settle in
    I don't play handball anymore
no more long hikes--no hunting
    or dancing till dawn--
still we go to a gym.

We go to the gym
    four times a week.
Treadmill--bicycle--stairmaster
    trying to beat the clock and
staying ahead of winter.

Even grandchildren help
    to push the clock back to
Springtime again.

. . .

NEW YEARS RESOLUTIONS--2002

TO BE MORE POSITIVE IN MY ATTITUDE

TO BE MORE ACTIVE WITH POETRY READINGS
AND ALL ACTIVITIES

TO BE ABLE TO WALK AND RETURN TO THE GYM

TO REMEMBER HOW VULNERABLE WE CAN BE
AND NEVER TAKE LIFE FOR GRANTED

TO LOOK FORWARD TO THE FIRST DAY OF THE
REST OF OUR LIVES TOGETHER--
LOVE YOU JEANNE.

. . .

A SENTINEL*

Indians walking through the forest
     carrying their kill--a deer
all the way to Mahwah--
     food for their people
while our tree--our sentinel
     watched.

Some trees are taken away
     to make room for new homes and
new people arriving.
     Still our tree remains
a sentinel in our forest.

It stands and watches
     the weather change--
leaves come and leaves go
     but our tree continues to grow
a sentinel in our forest.

. . .

*More than 32 feet in circumference
I call this mighty oak tree
The Sentinel.

WHAT WAS--WHAT IS--WHAT WILL BE

I used to remember
everyone that graduated High School
went to college--
joined the army--
got married and
even those that had to get married.

I used to remember
buying a new home--
buying a not so new car--
making new friends--
everyone with babies
baby sitters and
Saturday night movies.

I used to remember
children born--
Bar Mitzvahs--
weekends in the Catskills and
a life with family and friends.

Time marches on and
we don't talk about
who got married--
another Bar Mitzvah--
baby sitters.
We talk about Florida and
Senior Citizens.

Now I remember
every doctor in Rockland County--
friends that are sick--
pills that I take every day and
the name of a good chiropractor.

We go to a gym--
we are part of the gym--
these people are our friends and
once more we talk about
baby sitters--
what picture is playing in the movies--
where is the best college--

WHAT WAS--WHAT IS & WHAT WILL BE

HOLIDAYS

Presidents Day--
Washington and Lincoln combined--
Memorial Day parades and
July 4th--party time.

I used to look forward to
no work today--
sleeping late--a day of rest--
Holidays.

I don't look forward
to holidays anymore.
No work today--
sleeping late--a day of rest--
Now this is every day.

Retired--we sleep later
but we also go to sleep later.
No work today but
in the nights we play.

. . .

SPRING

Buds open
    mouths with no teeth and
spit out multi-colored flowers
    that smile at the sun.

Animals, all excited
    rush for fresh food
now available
    in their Spring supermarket.

New hungry families
    emerge from their winter homes
for an eating frenzy and
    to play.

Everything is new--
    it is a new year
for animals, flowers
    and for us too.

A blue year 2001--
    many problems but--
my leg is OK now and--
    we will walk to a great 2002.

. . .

<u>CAT</u>

There is a young cat from Siam
  never as fat as I am.
Tiffany is her name
  mischief is her game.
Food is her ploy
  to be used as a toy.
That is why she is so thin
  but for me, to waste food is a sin.

. . .

FINIS

It seems
there is no more poetry
left in me
only a world
gone beserk
violence--death
suicide bombers
destruction
and more death.
Children die and
mothers cry and
families disappear.

. . .

WAITING

The robin arrived
     showed his big red chest
then retired to search for and
     rebuild last years nest.

A chipmunk bleary eyed
     peaks at the sun
then scurries back to his home.
     It's too early for him.

I am waiting--
     for magnolia buds to open--
star burst blossoms bloom--
     and the aroma of spring should prevail.

I am waiting--
     for leaves to dress the trees
all in their green finery and
     a new year for them to begin.

I am waiting for
     another vacation and
grandchildren a year older and
     for us, another year to grow on.

I am waiting for peace
     in Afghanistan
     in Israel
     in the world.

.   .   .

HAIKU POETRY

Moon sleeping on lake
nothing stirs there is no sound
pebble wakes the moon.

Side by side
a man and his shadow
walk in moonlight.

Sign
on cemetery gate
available.

Lobster in tank
waiting for dinner
is dinner.

Undressed she shivers
as winter winds blow
the sickly elm.

Mosquito
in my shower
doesn't use soap.

Siamese cat
greets another siamese cat
with a hiss.

Buck
searches for doe
object fawn.

Moon shines
on large copper pot
moonshine.

Over the icy waves
the airplane flies
into tomorrow.

Standing and watching
the deer standing and watching
then he shoots.

. . .

OUR MAGNOLIA TREE

Squirrels attack
    large ripe buds--
a prelude to
    starburst blossoms.

Blossoms open and
    fill our area with color
and the aroma of spring.

An explosion of green--
    leaves cover our magnolia tree
forcing blossoms to depart
    preparing our tree for summer.

Only one--the last blossom
    seen from the center of
our livingroom window
    still reminds us of
a cooler springtime.

We prepare for
    an invasion of terrorists
death and destruction--
    our new way of life.

Preparedness, always ready
    we have to be alert as
we watch our last starburst
    thinking about yesterday
reminiscing about a quieter time.

Now, with new growth
    of flora and fauna and
the joy of spring
    we pray for the growth of
new thoughts--productive minds
    and a time of peace.

. . .

FARTING

Farting is a natural expression
     of guilt that you have
for eating something that
     you shouldn't have
that tastes so good
     and you knew that you could
but you really shouldn't have.

Farting is a natural expression
     announcing to friend and foe
that you were a bad boy
     and you know
that friend and foe
     will share in your guilt
and they will express
     --their opinion--

     YOU STINK.

.   .   .

GOBELDEGOOK

Away, I am going away
but I would rather stay
stay to go
away to stay
for another day
a day to stay
away, to go away.

. . .

THE LONG WAIT

There is no music
there is no television
only pictures adorn the walls.

Ernest Hemingway was hunting
crocodiles, baboons, ostriches
king cobras, tigers and more.

Now, only on chapter eight
I put the Hemingway book down
to rest my eyes and my nerves.

From this tenth floor window
a beautiful scene greets me--
the Hudson River in all of its glory.

George Washington Bridge
the most beautiful bridge
smiles at me.

Back to my seat and
once more my Hemingway book
and I wait and wait and wait.

There are seven pictures
each with a different scene
and a swan held by an older woman.

Finally the doctor returns--
the mammogram was negative.
Thank GOD.

. . .

ARTHUR AVENUE*

BARRELS ARE FULL OF
    OLIVES GREEN AND RED
SLEEPING IN A BRINY BED
    WITH PARMESAN CHEESE AT THE DOOR
GENOA SALAMI AND MORE--

A GLASS OF WINE ENHANCES--
    ODORS OF GARLIC, PASTA AND ALL.

--DIET--WHAT DIET--???

. . .

Arthur Avenue
The Bronx, New York

GOING HOME

Little bird in a tree
    walking back and forth impatiently
waiting to get back home.

How like the bird are we
    always rushing impatiently
arriving early--then we wait.

With a mouthful of food
    the little bird waits
for the obstruction (us) to go away.

He flies up and then
    down in a dive
returning to the same branch.

Little bird in a tree
    walks back and forth impatiently
still trying to get back home.

He stares at us
    complains to us and
demands that we move.

No longer able to wait
    the little bird flies to his nest--
his home in our bushes.

. . .

JUNE 24, 2002--10PM

She was HIS cat.
HE called her home
to sit on HIS right side.

An Angel, she did so much
to help us live our lives.
She woke us in the morning and
put us to sleep at night.

During the day
she spoke to us
of all things important to her.

Of course we could play games
but it was so important
to roll up in the crook of my leg
and sleep the afternoon away.

Twelve years of love--
unconditional love--
and all she asked in return
is just to be cared for and loved.

She is gone but
her essence remains.
Tiffany the beautiful Siamese cat
is still with us.

. . .

People that have not
     earned the love of an animal
nor enjoyed the love of an animal and
     people that do not
respect the space of an animal
     are people that
I do not want to know.
     They have not
and do not know
     how to live--to love.
They can never be
     a friend.

. . .

POST MORTEM

We stroked her dead body
trying to feel
one more purr.

There was movement
vibration
my hand was shaking
my heart was beating too fast
I was in shock
she could not be
she was too young
our beautiful Siamese Cat
she was dead.

She ate with us--

She slept with us--

She died alone..

. . .

I WISH

I wish that I
could paint with words
the splendors of this world
seen mainly by the birds.

The freedom of the whale
breaching on the horizon and
spouting at the moon.

I wish that I
could paint with words
the beauty and mystery
in the eyes of an owl.

The first robins of spring
joining the rabbits
cardinals and a scarlet tanager.

I wish that I
could paint with words
the greening of our world
intermixed with colors of spring.

Our star burst magnolia tree
in full bloom
its aroma permeating the area.

I wish that I
could describe with words
the caring and love
that a cat has for its family.

The caring and love
that we had for
Tiffany, our Siamese Cat.

I WISH Page 2

I wish that I
could describe with words
the joys of spring, summer
autumn and winter.

Trees buffeted
by a summer breeze and
a deer comes ambling by.

I wish that I
could paint with words--

. . .

A NIGHT IN PROVINCETOWN

Whales breaching and
     spouting at the sleeping moon
on the horizon
     while the wild beach rose
watching the scene
     closes its petals to sleep
and we return to our motel
     also to sleep.

All too soon the DC-3's
     airplanes of the past
from a very active airport
     will wake the flora and fauna
and a new day will begin.

How quick
     new days begin
and our vacation ends.

Cranberry bogs
     decorated by a border
of multi-colored wild roses
     with ring-billed gulls
flying overhead and
     adding color to the scene
greet us as we rise
     to get banana walnut pancakes
juice and coffee--
     our breakfast.

. . .

A WINTER NIGHTMARE

Five o'clock--the workday is over.
     Snow is falling and the roads are slick.
I worry about the long, steep hill
     which I must descend to get home.

Moving slowly and smoothly
     I get through my first obstacle
a left turn to the main road
     on a slippery incline.

I hold my breath
     as I drive uphill
fearing that I will get stuck
     at the traffic light on top of the hill.

Strange--the light is out
     in fact it is not even there!
The snow is now heavy
     and the road has narrowed down.

High walls of snow
    bank each side of the road
blocking all houses from view.
    Where did all the cars go?

I approach the dreaded hill, and
    the car whizzes down
completely out of control
    like a drop on a rollercoaster.

The street into which I must turn
    is no longer visible.
White, only white surrounds me
    on the road and on the sides.

I must get to the drugstore
    to telephone my family.
Alone, the only car on the road
    I slowly ride into town.

But there is no town, no stores!
    Main street does not exist!
People mull around staring.
    They are dressed in heavy furs.

I stop the car and open the door.
    Artic air and wind assail me.
Some fur-clad men climb on the car
    bouncing it up and down.

I slam the door
    and turn on the ignition.
Just as the car is about to capsize
    the scene changes.

I'm in our own driveway
    behind the wheel of the car.
The clock tells me it is 5:30 P.M.
    I've just returned
from "The Twilight Zone".

. . .

A CHILDRENS VIEW OF CHRISTMAS EVE

'Twas the night before Christmas, and
    the house is a-bustling
Momma's in the kitchen cooking, baking
    and hustling.
Daddy comes home
    with his daily complaint:
The Tappan Zee Bridge is one
    great big pain.
Stuck for one half-hour on the span
    in his car
He would take the Bear Mountain Bridge
    if it weren't so far.

We children are told
    to go to our beds
and to try to have pleasant thoughts
    buzzing in our heads.
We hang up our stockings
    wishing with heart and soul
That we will find goodies
    and not sooty coal.

Putnam, Westchester and Rockland
    look festive and bright
lit up with colorful Christmas
    and Chanuka lights.
New City is a credit
    to the Rockland County Seat
with decorations at the courthouse
    and all along Main Street.
Cold Springs, reminiscent of yesteryear
    is a town to be picketed
on Sunday if parked past 2:30 P.M.
    your car will be ticketed.

A CHILDRENS VIEW OF CHRISTMAS EVE

Through the blinds shines
an eerie red glow
It gives the appearance of sequins
gleaming in the snow.
In the sky is a team of reindeer
and a sleigh
Santa took Rudolph with him
to help lead the way.
Fortified from house to house
with cake, cookies and milk
The Old Man makes his deliveries
run as smooth as silk.
The sleigh is now empty
there is nothing left on it
And it flies through the sky
at the speed of a comet
But a voice cuts through
the pre-dawn air
"Happy holidays, good health
and good cheer
and be kind to each other
throughout the year."

. . .

THE VISITOR

It was a January Sunday
     the sky was cloudy and hazy
a cold windy winter day
     good to stay home and be lazy.

Down in the basement there was a commotion
     our daughter was yelling and stuttering.
What the cause was, I had no notion, but
     then I heard the sound of wings fluttering.

I put aside my book and ran downstairs
     our cat ran in circles and let out a howl
I chased her up and calmed her fears.
     On the workbench was perched an owl!

It had yellow citrine eyes
     and a gray rippled chest.
A perpetual scowl made it look so wise
     In the avian family
this beauty was among the best.

We must release this wild critter
     it belongs in the fields and the trees
but not until we take its picture
     then through the window
he will fly in the breeze.

Through the chimney this bird entered our house
     I hope we will see it again.
Much excitement he did arouse
     in our woods perhaps
it will appear now and then.

SEASONAL MOODS

Wintertime
gray skies
skeletal trees
snow and sleet
ice and slush
short days and sadness.
Winter colors me blue.

Springtime
forsythias, magnolias, daffodils
new buds
birds nesting
sunshine and gentle rain
baseball.
Spring colors me pastel pink.

Summertime
brilliant blue skies
booming thunderstorms
lush green foliage
animals feasting
sunny beaches.
Summer colors me gold.

Autumntime
bright starry nights
leaves of orange, yellow and red
pumpkins and gourds
Halloween and Thanksgiving
football.
Autumn colors me bronze.

Blue, pink, gold, bronze--then blue again.

. . .

To Jack, Jean, Janet, Phil and Wendy--

My Poetic Friends

ANOTHER SUNDAY

An ordinary winter Sunday
    that happens to be my birthday.
We meet our poetic friends
    at the nursing home
and have a rewarding reading.

To these people, this is what I have to say:

Thank you for making my birthday
    a real pleasure,
The book of love poems and the calendar
    I will always treasure.
You are like stars in the firmament above
    radiating your warmth and love.

From all directions, north or south
    or east or west
you are "the creme de la creme,"
    the very best.

. . .

Jeanne Slavin Siegel

STORMY MEDITATIONS

Sitting on the boardwalk
    inside an open pavilion
I watch white frothy foam
    in the thrashing ocean.

Black nimbus clouds collect
    thunder begins to rumble, and,
two jagged streaks of lightning
    shoot across the sky.

Heavy drops of rain fall
    as the wind pushes the clouds
furiously through the sky.
    I run to seek secure shelter.

Suddenly what was familiar territory
    becomes very strange.
There are no more small stores
    or friendly homes I once knew.

Wind and sheets of rain
    tear at me as I run.
Music is heard through the fury
    chords and heavy bass octaves.

The strains of Liszt's "Mephisto Waltz"
    accompanies the storm,
then the melody of cajoling and pleading joins.
    Perhaps Mephistopheles is seeking
a new soul to own.

The rain slows down and
    the sun breaks through the clouds.
A rainbow arches across the sky
    as the music changes to
Chopin's "Fantasy Impromptu".

My book lies on the floor and
    our cat is curled in my lap.
I sit on the livingroom couch
    while the radio softly plays on.

. . .

ANTICIPATION

It is dark, windy and rainy
      will we be able to fly?
We kiss our daughter and hug our cat
      as the limo comes to drive us away.

It is raining in sheets
      as we taxi to the runway.
We ride-and ride-and ride--
      all on the ground.

At last we stop then
      we wait-and wait-and wait--
forty planes are ahead of us.
      We take off, only two hours late.

We fly in turbulence
      and we land in turbulence.
Manchester is cold, windy and rainy
      this is where we came in.

.   .   .

THE ARRIVAL

A mixed-up taxi driver
    cannot find our son's home.
He scrutinizes a map
    while the meter runs on.

We arrive and a small blond princess
    throws her arms around us
followed by her handsome brother
    and their Dad and Mother.

"Rainbow", the tortoise shell tabby
    ambles in to greet us.
We are tired and jet-lagged
    but we are with our family.

. . .

THE ROUTINE

Jet lag--five hours lost, and
    a sixth hour added
with the advent of their daylight time.
    However, there is no time to be tired.

Six thirty in the morning-
    a seven year old princess
and a five year old prince
    jump into our bed to play.

Time to begin the day.
    The children on new scooters
and the adults on foot
    are ready to go into town.

We browse the stores
    in the walking mall, and
lunch at our daily stop--McDonald's.
    Then it's on to the market, and home.

The weather is cold and wet
    but the manicured lawns are green.
Crocuses, daffodils and forsythias
    are in full bloom.

Small neat homes line the street.
    Children ride scooters and play
while people attend to their chores--
    a picture of suburban peace.

. . .

THE DEPARTURE

All vacations must end, and
ours is winding down.
The day before we leave
we are blessed with sunshine.

In order to celebrate this happening
we take a train to Manchester.
We lunch on fish and chips
delicious and properly greasy.

We enjoy a delightful day
walking around this city
which has modern malls and stores
but old-fashioned trolley tracks.

Early the next morning
we say our goodbyes.
We hug the children and parents
then leave with some tears.

In my mind I relive the past ten days.
The plane trip is calm and smooth.
I anxiously await landing and
we miss our daughter,
our cat and our home.

We land and come home to--
guess what? Rain, wind and cold.
I miss our family overseas
but it is good to be home.

. . .

THE TREE FROM HELL

It must come from the Underworld
     transplanted from
the banks of the River Styx;
     a sight, hideous and grotesque
in a most unlikely place.

The bark is as black as pitch
     it has a crooked trunk.
Its branches are knobby and deformed
     as in a horror movie scene.

The top is completely barren
     with small offshoots of twigs
resembling skeletal claws
     reaching up to the sky.

About halfway down
     green slimy willow fronds
drip down toward the ground
     keeping contact with Hades below.

Among the birds only the crow
     will perch on these cursed branches.
He stares and catches a passerby's eye
     then caws and warbles, "Nevermore"*.

This weird semblance of a tree
     stands in the rear of a busy area.
People attend to their daily chores--
     next to the gate to Hell.

*From "The Raven" by Edgar Allen Poe

. . .

IN A CLASS OF ITS OWN

It has a furry black body
adorned with two yellow stripes.
It floats gracefully from shrub to shrub
and from flower to flower
sometimes hovering in suspended animation.

Spreading diaphanous wings in flight
it soars through the air
buzzing a distinctive tune
described in musical composition
by Nicolai Rimsky-Korsakov*.

Unlike its relative of the yellow jacket
this insect gently moves about
cross pollinating the garden and
pleasing the eye of anyone
who will take time to observe its grace
and beauty.

*"The Flight of The Bumblebee"

• • •

THE STEREOTYPE

The time was the spring of 1943
   the place was Berlin, Germany.
Top Nazis were meeting in a room
   plotting who next
to send to their doom.

Outside birds and insects created a din
   inside music was being piped in.
One Nazi said, "Isn't that
   by Mendelsohn the Jew?"
Another exclaimed, "That can not be
   it will never do!"

Soldiers were called in--
   this must be stopped.
From their musical repertoire
   it will be dropped.
Mendelsohn's picture must come off the wall.
   Only pure Aryans were allowed after all!

One soldier said, "To remove it we're not able
   after all, none of them are labeled."
A leader answered,"This is easy to do.
   Remember you're talking about a Jew!
He had to be the ugliest, everyone knows.
   Besides he must have had a great big nose."

The soldiers went to work without delay
   the job had to be done
by the end of the day.
   Time wore on, it was getting late
when they came upon a certain portrait.

The man depicted had a dwarf-like head
   and a huge proboscis.
All concerned agreed that--
   there were none uglier than this.

The picture came down
   leaving a glaring space
for no longer on display
   was Richard Wagner's face.

. . .

A STERILE WORLD

Last night I had a nightmare.
Outdoors there were
only weeping willow trees,
no more maples, oaks or elms.
Even the evergreens ceased to exist.

Last night I had a nightmare.
The garden flowers were all begonias,
everywhere only in white.
No reds, no lavenders or pinks
brightened the landscape.

Last night I had a nightmare.
Even the birds were all the same--
only bluejays with cackling voices.
No more sparrows, robins or cardinals
added color and song to the air.

Last night I had a nightmare.
All the people had blond hair--
there were none with black,
brown or red tresses.
The men were all over six feet tall
and the women averaged
five feet nine inches.

Last night I had a nightmare.
Everybody had blue eyes--
there were no shades of brown,
hazel or green.
My dark eyed husband
son and grandson
had no place in this society.

Last night I had a nightmare.
Only one race existed--white.
There were no people of color
no black, no yellow
no red or brown--
all except pure Aryan types
were eliminated.

LAST NIGHT I HAD A NIGHTMARE.

. . .

TUESDAY, SEPTEMBER 11, 2001

How did it happen, where did we go wrong? This is the continental United States, the safest place in the world. Is complacency at fault? Our security in the air must be examined and tightened.

Our feelings about life have changed. None of us can be the same as before. After all the cliches and platitudes have been said, life must go on. Nations of the world must punish and put a stop to all terrorism. There can be no straddling the fence.

Through all this horror, we can take pride in our people, both as Americans and New Yorkers. Their selflessness and care for one another was heroic. We mourn the fire fighters, the police and all of the victims who have lost their lives. With all our hearts, we wish for the recovery of the injured.

Let us all pray in our own ways for comfort and consolation for the bereaved.

AND

May this day NEVER, EVER happen again.

. . .

CALIFORNIA--SUMMER IN THE DESERT

Santa Ana winds
     blow tumbleweed about
invading yards and blocking driveways
     as the morning sun burns down.

The desert floor is adorned
     with clumps of sagebrush.
Spiny Joshua trees
     inhabiting only the Mojave Desert
decorate this arid scene.
     Various cactus configurations
add green to the dun color.

In the distance snow can be seen
     capping the Sierra Nevadas
soon to be obliterated from view
     by the heavy oozing smog.

A line of rock upheaval
     in a northwesterly direction
marks the path of
     the San Andreas fault--
a disaster waiting to happen.

Certain cities along the coast
     have suffered periodic devastation
as earthquakes change the landscape.
     Is this state with all the scenic beauty
destined for oblivion
     like the lost continent of Atlantis?

. . .

HAIKU POETRY

Starry night
cicadas sing in chorus
one off key.

Flying high above
white cumulus clouds
I write High Ku.

White blossoms
on dogwood tree
bark at me.

Crow sits in snow
black bird
white ass.

Halloween costumes
next to Christmas display
where are the turkeys?

Bridge game over
happy winners--sore losers
no plum blossoms.

Man eating lunch with
cell phone glued to his ear
spills soup.

Black trunk and branches
slimy green willow fronds
and a crow.

Traffic jam
obscene gestures fly
in my direction.

Dawn breaks
birds chirp and my husband
snores.

Drizzle
distorted street lights
on the wet street.

GREAT EXPECTATIONS

It was December 31, 2000
      a few minutes before midnight.
I, along with my husband and friends
      held a glass of champagne.

On the large T-V screen
      we watched the ball on Times Square
descend slowly counting down
      the last ten seconds to 2001.

Happy New Year.
      We all hugged one another
and made a toast
      for all good things to come.

Winter moved out--
      the robin heralded Spring.
The barren trees got dressed and
      flowers burst into bloom.

We enjoyed the golden summer
      with calm complacency.
The terrorism of the Middle East
      was thousands of miles away.

Then came September 11th.
      Our worst nightmare was realized.
Terrorists demolished the Twin Towers
      and part of the Pentagon in Washington.

As the end of this year approaches
      apprehension becomes a part of life.
The possibility of bacterial warfare
      rears its ugly head.

The coming New Year
      will not be the same.
Naivete can no longer exist.
      As Americans we must rebuild
and get on with life.

•   •   •

FOREVER WINTER

Forsythias are in bloom.
     Dogwood, magnolias and cherry blossoms
add their color and fragrance
     to the outdoor scene.

At the crack of dawn
     birds sing their morning concert.
Light green leaves dress the trees, and
     lawns are turning to lush green.

The weather is warm--.
     Spring, the season of joy
has arrived --but--
     the gloom of winter still remains.

Clouds cover our existence.
     Suicide bombers, fanatics and terrorists
threaten life in the United States
     and all over the world.

Rudeness rules the highway.
     The prevalence of road rage
has reached an all time high.
     Courtesy is a rarity.

We must work together
     for a return to sanity.
Let us all pray for peace, and
     may spring come again.

. . .

A DECEMBER NIGHTMARE

Shards of glass--
     broken windows and
a shattered windshield.

Being removed from the car
     by EMS workers
into an ambulance.

My husband's bleeding head--
     doctors and nurses--
in the hospital.

Examinations--
     X-Rays --- Cat Scans and
treatment of wounds.

Our daughter and
     caring friends
all here with us.

Painful bruises--
     car destroyed--
no dream, reality.

A dreadful accident but
     we are alive.
Thank God.

. . .

FOR GRANDPA

What are heavy?
      sea, sand and sorrow.
What are brief?
      today and tomorrow.
What are frail?
      spring blossoms and youth.
What are deep?
      the ocean and truth.

By Skye & Jake Siegel

June 20, 2002

FOR GRANDMA

Is the moon tired?
      she looks so pale
within her misty veil
      she sails east to west
and takes no rest.
      Before the coming of the night
the moon shows papery white.
      Before the dawning of the day
she fades away.

By Skye & Jake Siegel

June 20, 2002

Skye is 8 years old

Jake is 6 years old

AUGUST 14, 1990--JUNE 24, 2002

She was a person--a fur person.
     She was all love and gentility.
She gave nothing but love and care
     asking nothing more than
our love in return.

She looked at you with expressive blue eyes
     knowing if you were happy or sad.
She cuddled and comforted by snuggling
     and putting her delicate front paws
on your hand.

When stroking her silky fur she purred
     showing her pleasure.
She had her playful times enjoying peek-a-boo
     and throwing toys and balls in the air.
She had love for her family
     her birth mother and her sister.

On June 24, 2002 she was called
     back to Heaven.
She was loaned to us for almost twelve years
     to give us comfort, help and love.

Now there is an empty space in our lives
     but her presence still is in the air.
Tiffany, you will always be with us.

.   .   .

1941

On a cold Sunday in New York City
my parents and I freeze in line
outside the Radio City Music Hall.

We finally are seated inside
enjoying a movie--
the Christmas show and the Rockettes.

England and Germany are at war.
This show affords some escape
from the bad news in the world.

I being a self-centered child
pay scant attention to the news.
This is all far away.

We leave the theater.
People are clustered around restaurants
listening to the radio.

Faces seem dazed and shocked
some have tears in their eyes.
What can be wrong?

We arrive at Times Square
and look at the news bulletin.
Our nation has been attacked.

This is that fateful day--
December 7, 1941.

. . .

THE ROSES OF CAPE COD

Crossing the Bourne Bridge
   we enter into the land of Cape Cod.
Riding along Route 6
   I look for the roses always present
in the month of July.
   Each side of the road is covered
by woods-but-where are the roses?

We ride through Sandwich,
   Cotuit and Barnstable
crossing over to Route 28
   and into Hyannis.
Here there are petunias, tiger lilies and
   yuccas-but-where are the roses?

Arriving at our motel in West Yarmouth
   there are more petunias, tiger lilies,
yuccas and a few daisies-but-
   where are the roses?

I feel disappointed, almost cheated.
   Then we go to dinner in Hyannis and
I spy a bunch of cultivated pink roses.
   My spirits rise slightly.

The next morning we ride along Route 28
   There I see wild roses
growing along fences
   some are in fields
or near cranberry bogs.
   Others, adorning the motels
are cultivated.

I see pink, white, yellow and
   reddish-orange roses.
Then, at last, comes
   the piece-de-resistance-
a huge bush of
   bright red American beauties.

These lovely flowers with their sweet aroma
   will be gone by August.
Other flora will take their place
   but I am happy to enjoy
the beauty of Cape Cod and its roses
   in the glorious month of July.

TREASURES OF THE PAST

The odor of age assails me
    as I enter the antique bookstore.
This shop in Cape Cod
    is set up like a huge library.

In the classical music section
    I can see Mozart
conduct "The Magic Flute".

Examining the libretto of
    "Tristan and Isolde",
I picture Wagner composing
    under dim light.

In the opera biography area
    I can hear Enrico Caruso
sing "Pagliacci".

Great performances of the past
    come to life in opera houses
all around the world.

I then come upon the old American poets
    reaquainting myself with Longfellow
Poe and others.

Finally I come to the mysteries
    rubbing elbows with
Sherlock Holmes and Sam Spade.
    How can I resist my childhood friend
Nancy Drew?

It's time to leave the past and
    to walk outside
back to the present
    taking with me some treasures
from long ago.

. . .

SEARCH AND FIND

The past returns to us
    in books from yesteryear
as we rummage
    in an antique bookstore.

Reading poetry that was written
    so long ago
even the odor of the past
    fills my nostrils.

Their life story--
    the way things were
unfolds before my eyes
    in a panoramic view
and I return to them
    only for a moment.

We take their book--
    their story
home with us
    to dream again.

.   .   .

ANOTHER TIME--ANOTHER PLACE

I am trying to talk
    to animals and trees
about life and love
    and a world that is free.

Our magnolia tree
    born in 1958 and
murdered in 1988--
    cut down in its prime
only thirty years old.

It was not enough time
    there was more life to live.

From a bud--a seed--
    a part of the tree--
it gave birth--rebirth.

Born again in 1989 and
    now, once more fully grown--
it survives
    growing taller
trying to reach the sky
    while squirrels are nourished
by its new buds
    before they are burst.

Behemoth clouds swim
    in a cerulean blue sky
over animals and trees and
    traffic on the Tappan Zee Bridge.

Days go by so fast
    years too--
even our cat that
    shared the birth and growth
of our magnolia tree
    is no longer with us.

How did our cat get into this poem?
    She is still with us
her essence hasn't left yet.

ANOTHER TIME--ANOTHER PLACE

Memories from another time--
    another place--
invade my thoughts.

Once more thinking about
    vacations in Europe--Israel--
and afraid to leave this country--
    terrorists everywhere
destroy our mindset--
    our way of life.

Now our vacations and
    even Tiffany our cat
all return to us
    in our poetry.

. . .

A PENNY POSTCARD--A BOOK--A LIFE

A penny postcard
a long important
means of communication
brought families together.

Holidays--reunions
short messages
became the norm.

World War 11 and
a shortage of paper
caused a new invention--
"V" mail and
more short messages.

I bought a new novel--
three hundred pages--
a penny a page--
thirty cents for the book.

World War 11 ended and
a new war began.
Inflation attacked.

A penny postcard
now twenty three cents and
a thirty cent novel
now thirty five dollars and
a seven hundred dollar new car
now twenty five thousand dollars.

Korea--Vietnam--
Middle East ongoing--
three wars later
everything is different.

No more "V" mail.
Now we have "E" mail
and Fax is still faster.

A PENNY POSTCARD--A BOOK--A LIFE

Shorter messages--
     less to read
when your computer
     is up to speed.

So much more to do and
     so much less that we can do.
Grandchildren we love to visit
     Skye, Jake, Christopher and
even Rainbow the cat.

No more handball
     against the wall
only a computer that
     we don't understand at all.

Business is down
     but we are not.

We write our poetry
     to remind the world--
we had a life to live and
     we did it well.

Still going strong
     we go to a gym
talk to young people and
     try to stay slim.

.   /   .